What's it Like to Work with a Police Dog?

Gill Munton

Contents

When were police dogs first used? 2

Which dogs make the best police dogs? 3

What do police dogs do? 4

Where do police dogs come from? 6

How are police dogs trained? 9

How much does it cost to train a police dog? 15

Index 16

OXFORD

UNIVERSITY PRESS

When were police dogs first used?

The Germans used dogs in World War I.
German shepherd dogs took messages and
guarded buildings.

The first police dogs in London started
work in 1938.

FACT BOX

German shepherd dogs are
also known as Alsatians.

Which dogs make the best police dogs?

German shepherd dogs make good police dogs. They are clever and loyal.

Buck is a German shepherd dog.

Other dogs are used too:

- Labradors
- golden retrievers
- springer spaniels.

Gipsy *(left)* is a Labrador.
Tosh *(right)* is a springer spaniel.

What do police dogs do?

Dogs have a strong sense of smell.
Police dogs use this to find drugs, guns,
bombs and dead bodies.

A police dog looks for hidden drugs.

They help to find lost property. They also track people.

Police dogs are trained to work with crowds. They help police at football matches and riots.

Police dogs are trained so they are not afraid of noise or crowds of people.

Where do police dogs come from?

Some police dogs are bred at the Dog Training
Establishment at Keston in Kent.

Every puppy stays at Keston until it is
eight weeks old. Then it is paired up with a
police officer. The puppy goes to live with
the officer at home.

A dog comes back to stay at Keston if:

- it is ill
- its handler is away.

The dogs are groomed every day. Grooming keeps their fur clean and healthy.

Buck enjoys being groomed.

All the dogs have their
own special food.

The vet comes to Keston twice a week.

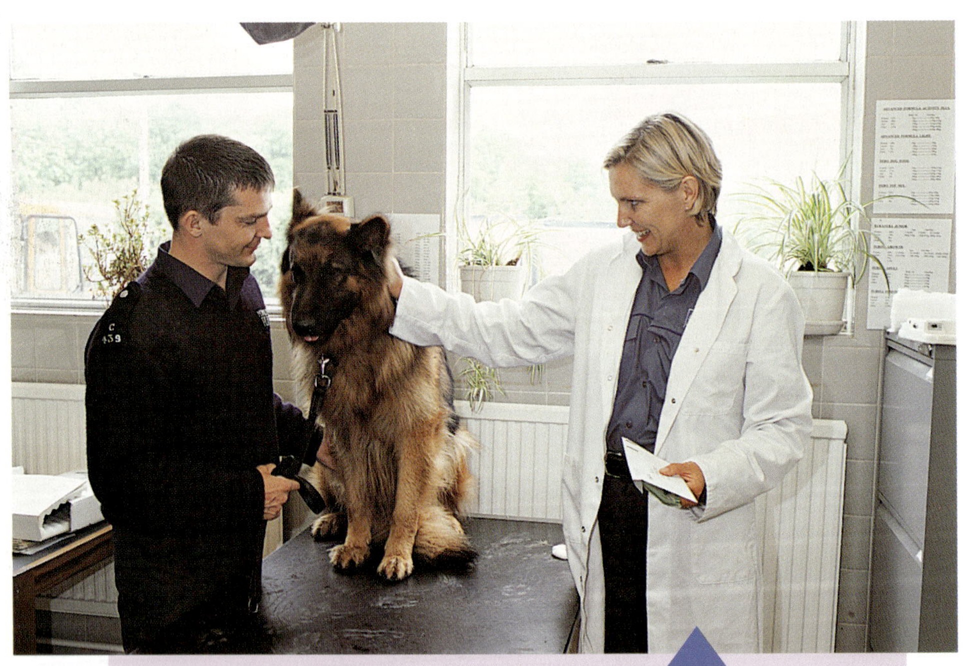

The vet is giving Bear a check-up. His
handler, Chris, stays with him all the time.

How are police dogs trained?

Training starts when the dog is 12 weeks old. It goes on for ten months. The dog learns to do what it is told.

When the dog does something right it gets a reward – and a pat!

First, the dog learns how to chase a person.
Then it learns how to stop them, by grabbing
their arm.

The trainer wears a special hard sleeve.
It is called a "bite bar" and it stops the
dog hurting the trainer's arm.

Next, the dog learns how to climb and jump.

By the end of the training, the dog can jump over a wall 1.85 metres high.

Some dogs learn how to find bombs. They use their strong sense of smell to sniff out the bomb.

1 The dog picks up the smell.

2 The smell leads to a bunker.

3 The handler opens the lid.

4 He finds the powder for a bomb.

Some dogs learn how to track people. They do this by following the person's smell.

Some dogs learn how to find guns. They learn
to search silently, then bark when they find
the gun.

This dog has found a gun in a tree.

How much does it cost to train a police dog?

In 2000 it cost £10,000 to train a police dog.

Index

Alsatian   2
bite bar   10
bombs   4, 12
drugs   4
food   8
football matches   5
German shepherd   2, 3
golden retriever   3
grooming   7
guns   4, 14
handler   7, 8
Keston   6, 7, 8
Labrador   2, 3
puppy   6
riots   5
springer spaniel   3
tracking   5, 13
training   9–15
vet   8
World War I   2